A Diamond

A Journey through Childhood Mental Illness

Melanie Burnell

live it
PUBLISHING

PRAISE FOR MELANIE BURNELL

'The Day My Head Slipped Out of my Head'... is a story that everybody will be interested in and should be shared with the world for interest and educational purposes.

HELENA CHARD, SKY TV CORRESPONDENT

Psychosis is not a straight forward subject and although Mel's story is easy to read, it should not be taken lightly. This mental illness grips the lives of many confident and successful adults unannounced, leaving them completely unprepared for the journey they are about to encounter.

... this book needed to be written, for it is about putting psychosis on the map in an accessible way so that no sufferer goes unnoticed, unhelped or misunderstood ever again.

If no-one is made aware how can we help?

NAOMI PHELAN MA

This book is dedicated to my special girl,

Riannon

"You're going to be happy," said Life.
"But first I'll make you strong."

Chapter One

Logalosh...

My little 'Logalosh' was born on 01.03.01.

I've always thought her easy-to-remember birth date was decided by the gods so I wouldn't forget it as my memory is not the best!

Loggy – real name Riannon - was so named as while she was waiting for my breast milk to come in, she made this cute little sound as she cried out: 'loga-loga-loga-loga!'

It really was sweet and in fact once the milk came (finally on day 5), she hardly ever cried again. She was, however, known from then on as my little Logalosh!

I was only 19 years old when I had her. I had enjoyed my pregnancy and felt an overwhelming maternal love right from the moment I found out I was pregnant which grew stronger with every passing day. From the second I laid eyes on her, it was like I couldn't remember a time when she wasn't part of my life.

We immediately had a special bond, I couldn't stop cuddling and looking at her. I remember how much I loved her 'new' smell… it was intoxicating! It felt like she was a gift and I felt blessed to have her.

Just two weeks later, I split from her dad, Jamie. He too was young and despite my best efforts, he wasn't interested in being a family. He wanted to go out drinking and partying, not stay in with a baby, so we parted ways amicably.

We hadn't been together long when I fell pregnant and I knew that him leaving had been on the cards for some time. Yet I felt incredibly positive about my future with my baby. I felt strong and knew no different, so I embraced the situation.

I was young, optimistic and headstrong. I had thought, perhaps naively, that having a baby would complete me somehow and be just like having a real-life doll. In fact, the reality was pretty much that!

I was blessed with an adorable, cute little baby who slept all night and contentedly cooed all day. After years of partying and reckless teenage behaviour, I had finally grown up and being a mother made me the happiest I'd ever been.

I made us a cosy home in the little ground floor flat that the council had allocated to me on the outskirts of town. It was my very first home after moving out of my parent's house and I took such pride in decorating and cleaning it. I didn't have much money, so would go shopping in the charity shops and car boot sales for nice home-ware knickknacks and baby clothes. I bought fresh healthy food which I enjoyed cooking for us both.

Every day, I would walk Riannon into town in her pram to meet my friend Claire who was the same age as me. We had met at antenatal classes and she'd had her baby, Leo, on the same day I'd had Riannon. I felt a bit sorry for her as she really had her hands full with Leo, who didn't sleep much and cried a lot.

She loved seeing Riannon, always holding her and playing with her. I realised how lucky I was to have such a good baby and how different it could have been.

One day, when we were on our way into town it was raining, so I pulled up the pram hood and rain shield when suddenly a little hand appeared, pulling down the fabric slightly, revealing big beady eyes staring at me and a cheeky smile - how cute!

I fed Riannon on demand for almost a year, which I found relaxing and bond-strengthening; it felt like the most natural thing in the world. Her weight chart went up in a perfectly straight line – something my health visitor had not seen before! I was so proud and delighted at how much I was enjoying motherhood.

After the initial shock of my pregnancy, my parents were very supportive and they too doted on the baby. As a very close family, my mum, dad and younger sister Caz, played a huge part in her upbringing and I felt very lucky to have them. They lived nearby, so we often went round there for dinner or even to stay sometimes; Riannon had her own room in their house!

We all went abroad on family holidays and enjoyed many lovely meals and days out together. Riannon was the apple of all our eyes which, being my only child and my parent's only grandchild, is understandable!

Before long, she had grown into a bright, sociable and happy toddler. Her dad stayed on the peripheral of her life. As time went on he gradually saw a bit more of her, which I encouraged. It was important to me that she knew her dad, even though she didn't see him very often.

When Riannon was nine months old, we were lucky to have been moved to a bigger flat in a lovely rural village, just five minutes from where my parents lived. There were only four flats to each building and ours was ground floor, backing onto a huge south-facing garden. It was very spacious and we had lovely neighbours, who we quickly grew close to.

Jane was ten years older than me and lived opposite with her two teenage daughters, Petra and Zoe, both lovely girls who would babysit for Riannon when I occasionally went out with friends. Jane and I would often put the world to rights over a bottle of wine in the evenings round mine when Riannon was in bed.

Julie was twenty years older than me and lived above with her teenage son, Mark. She was one of the funniest women I had ever met, with the dirtiest mind! The three of us were always in each other's places and they both adored Riannon.

Julie used to host New Years Eve and Halloween parties, which Riannon loved. We called ourselves the 'Three Musketeers' as the only other person in our building was Jim, the old boy who lived above Jane. He kept himself to himself, but moaned about the bins now and again, if they weren't put back straight.

We were all happy, strong single mums, and we shared similar difficult pasts, which bonded us together. I had suffered from low self esteem as a young girl, following a long stint of bullying at school and was in an abusive relationship from the age of sixteen until just before I met Jamie. I looked to them as inspiration, as they too had come through difficult times and were stronger for it. Jane was my age when she'd had Petra and she had become such a balanced, happy teenager.

It gave me hope that Riannon could grow up the same, even though she wasn't from a traditional '2.4' two-parent family.

When Riannon had just turned three, I met Marcus, who was five years older than me, on a night out in Luton. I liked his genuine, kind nature and we got on really well. He was a lovely northern guy with a heart of gold and he made me very happy. It was my first relationship since Riannon's dad and when I felt the time was right to introduce him to Riannon, it was perfect.

He adored her and she adored him. He didn't have children and he treated her like his own. I asked him to move in after a few weeks.

He was a fire-fighter with lots of free time as he worked two days on, then two nights, then four days off. For the first time, I had a partner to help look after Riannon, which I found really helpful. He would take her to nursery, read her bedtime stories and make her breakfast. They really enjoyed each other's company and Riannon was a lot more affectionate with Marcus than I'd seen her with anyone else, including me. While they grew close, I found the time to start my own creative business, which I pursued passionately.

I enrolled on a business scheme where I went on courses to learn about sales, finance and marketing. I was awarded a Princes Trust grant, loan and mentor as a young person wanting to better myself. I developed a fierce ambition, working determinedly on trying to build a future for us all.

When Riannon was five, I was a finalist in the Shell Live Wire Young Entrepreneur of the Year awards. My business became very demanding as it grew. I started as an Interior Art Designer, creating bespoke artwork to suit client's décor in the era of 'Changing Rooms' where everyone was into decorating their homes! Within a few years I had my own little gallery representing 15 local artists. I would later go on to form a huge Arts Centre exhibiting work from over 200 artists, then create one of the world's leading online artist guides showcasing over 700 artists from around the world.

This came at a price though.

Meanwhile, Riannon was flourishing. She was doing well at nursery and then school. She had lots of friends, was well-rounded and sociable as well as bright and sensible. I affectionately referred to her as being like 'Saffy' from 'Ab Fab' – the studious, wise daughter of a creative, flighty mother (me!).

I had always been an on-the-go, energetic, somewhat scatty 'live in the moment' type of person, but since running my business I was more so – Marcus used to say I was like a creative whirlwind! While Riannon's friend's mums were forever reminding their children to do things, she was always reminding me; my friend Liz affectionately used to tease me that Riannon was like the mum! I was so proud of her and was secretly relieved that my child was so level-headed.

"Mummy I think it's time you got to bed, you have work tomorrow."

"Five more minutes? I'm just finishing this email."

"Mummy can you have my PE kit ready for Tuesday please?"

"Oh, gosh, right yes good point – now where did I put it?"

"Mummy you need to get my packed lunch stuff in for tomorrow."

"Oh, shit, yes! Thanks sweetheart!"

Riannon was wise beyond her years and academically she was three years ahead, excelling in every subject. She loved school and had a great circle of friends. She was always going to parties and having friends round for tea.

Her social life was better than mine!

Melanie Burnell

Chapter Two

Heartbreak

As happy as Marcus and I were – we rarely argued – I found that as time went on my feelings for him were changing.

I felt like we had more of a brother/sister type relationship rather than that of lovers. Maybe life just got in the way, but I couldn't shake the feeling that he wasn't 'the one.' I kept this to myself for a number of years, for Riannon's sake – they were so close and he was such a loving father figure. I knew if we broke up, it would break her heart and I desperately wanted to protect her from that.

When Riannon was seven, four and a half years after Marcus and I met, I had a long heart to heart with my mum and broke down, explaining everything to her. Talking it through made me realise it was wrong to continue the relationship based on how I was feeling.

I didn't take the decision lightly and plucked up the courage to tell him how I felt. He got upset, then angry.

"Why didn't you tell me this earlier?"

I explained that I was hoping my feelings would change.

He asked what we were to do next.

"I guess you move out," I said, feeling anxious about how this would affect Riannon. He didn't fight for me. He wasn't the most passionate of people and this just affirmed to me that I'd done the right thing – for me.

But how would it affect Riannon? I hoped that she would be ok in time, but I knew I was about to blow her world apart.

She was sat doing colouring in at the front room table. I sat down with her.

"I've got something to tell you sweetheart," I said softly.

I didn't know how to say it. I just held her hand and said: "Marcus and me are splitting up, I'm so sorry. It's not your fault, we just don't love each other anymore."

I'll never forget her face – she was heartbroken and just cried and cried. I felt so guilty and my stomach was in knots seeing her so upset. Marcus then surprised me by making a decision I hadn't expected. He felt it would be kinder to her – and him – to just cut contact with her. I begged him not to do this as I knew she felt rejected and confused, but he did.

He moved in to a friend's place then moved away and we never heard from him again.

She missed him so much she literally hurt.

This was the first time she had felt heartbreak. I felt awful that she was experiencing this at just seven years old. Her family and friends, teachers and I all rallied round to support her. I remember saying to her that this would make her stronger in the future – that if she could be this hurt and survive and heal, she would be able to deal with anything that life threw at her. She kept photos of him and I think she internalised her feelings as she couldn't talk about him.

She wasn't one to talk much about her feelings in general – a trait from her father – but she knew I was there to talk to any time she wanted. I'm very open and affectionate - my whole family are. Riannon, on the other hand, doesn't give much away, so it's hard to know what she's thinking a lot of the time.

I just knew that she would never forget him and it would still hurt her deeply many years after.

Thankfully it wasn't long before I heard her laughing again and she continued to do well at school and had a wide circle of lovely friends. I kept praying that my love for her would help heal her. It certainly seemed to as time went on.

I made sure our home was a happy one, with regular girlie nights watching movies with popcorn, lots of laughing, 'make your own pizza' nights and shopping trips (retail therapy!) Riannon was always a very girlie-girl, loving makeup and clothes, so we had lots of fun experimenting with these things together.

Just as I hadn't bargained for Marcus to cut Riannon out of his life, something else I hadn't expected to come out of this was that her dad now wanted to see more of her.

Maybe he felt he couldn't get too involved while I was with Marcus – it could have been a 'guy thing' perhaps?! But soon after Marcus left, her dad got back in touch they started seeing each other regularly, building their own relationship which I was really grateful for.

Jamie hadn't had another relationship since me and I got the impression he regretted being so wayward all those years earlier, missing out on being a family with us. As a person he had grown up, wasn't drinking and partying as much as before and we started spending time together, which was nice for Riannon. He accepted that I didn't want to be in a relationship with him, but we became friends and we would spend the weekends at mine, the three of us watching Saturday night TV together – he would even stay over, on the sofa sometimes!

It was a nice set up as Riannon had both her mum and dad around. She once said she wished we would get back together, but I explained that we didn't have those feelings for each other, that we were better and happier as friends. I had started online dating and Jamie used to look after Riannon while I went out on dates! Then I would come back and tell them both all about it, making them laugh with all the funny stories I told them. I didn't dedicate a huge amount of time to dating, but was hopeful that I would meet my Mr Right one day and was enjoying meeting new people along the way.

Riannon used to help me look through their online profiles and I even set Jamie up on a few dates, which was pretty good going as he was so shy – I used to message the girls on his behalf!

These were fun times and Riannon and I were happy.

Chapter Three

Breakdown

When Riannon was almost eight, I opened a small gallery tucked away in a converted barn in a quaint village a few miles away.

Riannon was proud of me and I enjoyed making it a gorgeous destination for local art lovers. I soon outgrew the premises and a year later, I embarked on my biggest project yet. I opened a huge four-gallery Arts Centre in the busy centre of a nearby town with a business partner and eleven staff.

I saw less of Jamie as I now worked weekends, but he still saw Riannon.

Over the next two years, I worked tirelessly to try to make my business a success. Sadly, this came at the expense of my health, my social life and my relationships with friends and family. Riannon would be telling me about her day at school and all I could think about was selling more gallery space to artists to meet our outgoings that month.

My partner and I weren't taking any money from the business as our overheads were so high. I would snap at my parents when they questioned why I was doing all this with nothing to show for it. It was a really stressful time and I was smoking and drinking a lot to help deal with the stress which caused me to lose weight rapidly. I was tearful and anxious, so the doctor prescribed me anti-depressants.

Riannon must have known how stressed I was, but she never showed any signs of being affected, taking it all in her stride, focussing on her school work and friendships and always being loving and kind towards me, which I cherished.

* * *

During half term, Riannon would come with me to the centre, helping to laminate posters and hang artwork, which she loved. While she continued to do well at school and at home, my family grew increasingly concerned about me - my weight-loss, stress levels and the hours I was working were all signs that something wasn't right.

My neighbours Jane and Julie, had both moved out of the building so the reassuring tight-knit circle around me at home had got smaller. I had also met someone online, Richard, who was a lot older than me at nearly fifty. He was overbearing, a bit controlling and almost obsessive over me.

I was quite vulnerable as I was emotionally drained from all the stress of work, so things progressed further with him than they might have had I been fit and fighting strong mentally.

I introduced him to Riannon and we started staying over at his at weekends. Things at work were becoming more difficult as I knew the centre was close to folding, so I began working ferociously through the night on an even bigger project that I was convinced would finally set Riannon and I up for the future – a global website for artists.

I had pressure from all my artists, my business partner and my staff to make the transition from centre to online before we lost everything. My stress levels were through the roof. I lived and breathed that centre and website, and in December 2011 just as we had to close the centre, the site was ready for launch in the New Year. I had done it!

But at what cost?

* * *

It was Christmas and I tried to be happy and smiley for the sake of Riannon, now ten, Richard and my family. But I was a shadow of my former self and I was really scared.

My parents and Richard were so worried about me, so Riannon must have been. I couldn't think straight or hold a conversation and began to have panic attacks when I was out. I had lost more weight and was now unable to sleep.

I knew something was seriously wrong, but didn't know what it was or what to do about it. I couldn't work as I couldn't even write a simple email, so my business partner phased me out the business. I didn't even care much though, I was so ill I just wanted to feel normal again.

I was in a desperate place where I genuinely felt there

was no hope of me recovering from whatever I 'had.' I was actually experiencing psychosis, a severe mental illness – a breakdown of sorts, caused by all the stress, but the doctors and psychiatrists did not pick up on this until it was almost too late.

I was now in the grips of psychosis, and can remember getting really angry at one point with Riannon, grabbing myself by the neck and screaming "I want to die!" But most of the following few months were a blur... of just wanting to die.

This is Riannon's account of what she was thinking...

(Extract from 'The Day My Brain Slipped Out My Head and Onto The Kitchen Floor by Melanie Burnell)

"
Over 7 months I literally watched my mum change in front of my eyes... She started off by being as happy as life could be... Then moments later she would turn into the complete opposite. It was like she had an angel on one shoulder and a devil on the other.

After a few months of being like that there was a big downfall it was like the devil defeated the angel... She just turned into someone who couldn't think... You could tell she couldn't think because her eyes would always look confused if you said anything and it would always take a while for her to understand anything that you would say. I never knew why she was like this, I just thought it was a phase but it went on for far too long. I was so worried and frustrated rolled into one why she was being like this. I didn't like the person she turned into… Someone who couldn't walk up the stairs or even do the simplest things like making a sandwich.

At that time I never really understood what was happening; I did a lot for myself, the rest either my Nan or Richard did. Most of the time my mum would be very frail and extremely weak, Richard did most things for her to let her relax; I remember one night my mum grabbed herself by the scruff of the neck and threatened to kill herself right there at that moment. Life was hard but I never thought it would end up the way it did."

On the night of March 31st 2012, unable to cope anymore and not thinking straight, I took a cocktail of pills at Richard's house while he was out with Riannon buying pens from a late night supermarket so she could finish her homework.

I scribbled a goodbye note to Riannon and went to sleep, relieved that I would not wake up.

I stumbled out of bed some time later, unable to stand or speak properly, just making noises and foaming at the mouth. Richard was in Riannon's room reading her a bedtime story and they came out to see what the noise was.

This is Riannon's account of what she saw…

(Extract from 'The Day My Brain Slipped Out My Head and Onto The Kitchen Floor by Melanie Burnell)

" We heard a weird sound that came from the hallway... 'MMM' and then a loud stumble... Richard gently said 'wait there.' Of course I stuck my head out to see what was happening and standing there in front of my very eyes was my mum with white all around her mouth making the same groany sound... Her dark chocolate eyes looked half dead as they twitched along with the rest of her face... She tried to speak but all that came out were horrible sounds that I still remember today, the image I saw was just horrific... Richard kept asking questions like 'Mel what have you done, what's happening?' And the only response he got was 'TABLETS' In an out of breath tone, Richard's face drained as he tried to act strong but inside he was dying; just like I thought my mum was! Whilst Richard was asking all these questions he was resting my mum on the bed and on the phone to the ambulance.

A few moments later the doorbell rang and the most complicated door I ever saw in my life stood before me locked in all types of different ways... I was scared I would take too long to open the door and it would be too late... she would be dead. Somehow I opened the door and the ambulance crew rushed upstairs and took my mum away as a young nurse was calming me and reassuring me it was going to be alright... I had no idea what was going on as my face froze with icy tears rolling down my cheeks, as the ambulance took my mum away me and Richard followed straight to the hospital.

I remember falling asleep on his lap with tears still

rolling down my face. Maybe around the time of 2 or 3 in the morning they let me see my mum… they led us both into a curtain closed room with my mum laying there with tubes surrounding her. I watched Richard wipe away a tear as he stared at my mum who was fighting for her life.

She then got moved to another part of the hospital. I remember waking up on the floor with coats all around me, and seeing my auntie rushing in and taking me to Burger King and she tried to change the subject."

I survived, luckily. Not that I felt lucky at the time.

I wanted to die and I'm just so thankful that the psychiatrist I saw in that hospital referred me to a secure psychiatric ward where I stayed for three months - not that I was grateful at the time. I was petrified!

While I was in hospital, Riannon stayed with my parents. She seemed to deal with it all so well, even taking her SATS at school and passing every subject with A* grades. The only thing that seemed slightly strange looking back was her neatness in her bedroom at Mum and Dad's house. She always was fairly neat and tidy, but Mum said she had an almost ritualistic routine of lining up all her teddy bears and cushions neatly at the end of her bed every day.

Riannon used to make me little books and pictures which she gave me when she came to visit. I made her little trinket boxes and keepsakes in my art therapy classes.

Riannon says of visiting me in hospital:

(Extract from 'The Day My Brain Slipped Out My Head and Onto The Kitchen Floor by Melanie Burnell)

"
I never liked visiting mum even though it was the only time I got to see her before she got leave, it was hard to get into the building because of all the locks and security and when we finally got in we had to sign a book with what times and stuff then we had to go through where all the other patients were; then into a small room where my mum would sit almost like she didn't want to be there but inside I knew she did, one time I remember when we said good bye she mouthed ' I will never see you again.' As tears filled up my eyes I decided to ignore it let it pass but inside I was wondering if it might be true..."

Chapter Four

Reunited

During my time in hospital I gradually stopped wanting to die and with the right diagnosis, medication and treatment, I'm delighted to say that I made a full recovery.

Three months to the day after admission, I was allowed to go home and was elated! It was as if a light switch had been turned back on inside my head and I felt I was back to my old self. I felt like I'd been given a second chance at life and couldn't wait to return to my flat and be back at home with Riannon.

Everyone rallied around me, making sure I was ok – my mum, my friends, Richard, my care support worker who I was allocated for the next three years to make sure I stayed well and didn't relapse.

Riannon seemed so happy to be back at home with me and we got back into the swing of things very easily. We were both so happy again. I made the decision to end things with Richard, as I felt he never knew the real me – just the 'me' who was very ill – and I was no longer that person.

Now I was better I didn't like his controlling ways and

didn't want to do what he said or think the way he wanted me to think.

I was back in control of my destiny and life was great again, just me and Loggy.

I had a new lease of life – I laughed harder, I smiled more and the world just seemed somehow more bright and colourful. I discovered social media, redecorated my flat, took good care of myself and focussed on me and Riannon again, like old times.

I started cooking again and spent quality time with my friends and family. As time went on, my hospital stay seemed like a distant memory and I focussed on staying well and being a good mum. Riannon was adorable; it was like living with a mate. She seemed so grown up, taking an interest in helping me cook and clean. My heart burst with pride at how well she had coped with everything and I couldn't help but tell her a hundred times a day how much I loved her and how proud I was of her.

She was growing into a young lady now; she was so tall and slender, with long dark blonde hair and a beautiful elfin face. I loved looking at her. She was so beautiful, which I told her often. It was important to me that she had confidence in herself which I tried to instil.

I was very open about what I had been through and it was talked about often as a family, as we all tried to make sense of it.

Riannon never really spoke much about her feelings or what she had been through, but she took an interest in the book I was writing about my experience. I was writing it as I felt strongly that more people needed to be made aware of psychosis and even discussed starting a charity with my care coordinator.

Documenting my experience was proving quite therapeutic and I was enjoying writing it. I decided on the title: '*The Day My Brain Slipped Out My Head and Onto The Kitchen Floor*' which Riannon thought was great! I had taken her on a girlie weekend city break and we were just chilling in our hotel bed after a day shopping when I started writing in my journal. She asked if she could write something too. I was so glad she was finally verbalising her feelings!

I handed her my pen and note book and she wrote away. It was upsetting to read, but I was so glad she was letting her feelings out and I included it all in my book. She was very proud of my journey and was delighted when it got published on Amazon.

I was even invited on the Chrissy B show to talk about it, which Riannon thought was amazing!

Not long after I left hospital, Riannon's dad, who had been supportive throughout my breakdown, had started seeing someone new called Karen. She had a daughter, Chloe who was Riannon's age. Riannon loved them to pieces and they all spent the weekends together, which I thought was really nice. Riannon used to tell me funny stories about her time with them and I was really happy that Jamie had finally met someone.

Sadly, about six months later their relationship ended and Riannon was understandably quite upset. I really felt for her and tried to cheer her up with funny movies and of course, chocolate!

She wasn't one to stay down for long and she soon bounced back, although I knew it still hurt her as she got teary now and again for some time after. It's always hard when your child is hurting and you are powerless to change the situation. I focussed on her upcoming twelfth birthday, where I organised a makeover party for her and her friends. My family have always made a big fuss of birthdays and Christmas for as long as I can remember back and I passed this tradition onto Riannon.

I decorated the whole flat with pink balloons and banners and bought her loads of presents and a big birthday badge. The girls all tried on my various glitzy dresses from back in my clubbing days, my high heels and accessories.

My mum, my sister Caz and I then styled each girls hair and makeup and we photographed them. I then edited the pictures in Photoshop with funky backgrounds and gave each girl a disc of images along with a goodie bag to take home.

The girls loved it! They had sparkling orange juice in long stemmed champagne glasses and lots of pizza.

I had made Riannon's cake every year for her birthday, apart from the previous year as I was so ill, I was unable to. Even though I tried, I just couldn't do it.

It felt great to be able to make it this year.

Riannon continued to thrive at school and at home and I started working part time on a new business venture with an old associate. It was an art website not dissimilar from my previous one, but this time I didn't have any of the stresses involved. There were no financial or time pressures and I enjoyed working on it from home, when it suited me.

Things were going great.

Melanie Burnell

Chapter Five

A Year To The Day

Almost a year to the day since leaving hospital, something really awful happened which changed everything.

It was about 10pm on a Monday evening in August 2013. I was sitting on the sofa, working on some new designs on my laptop for an upcoming email campaign to target more artists.

It had been a normal evening. Riannon had been chilling in her room after playing out with her friends. I'd heard her pottering about in the kitchen a little earlier, presumably making a cup of tea. The sound from the kitchen radio was quietly coming through, playing easy listening songs when suddenly Riannon breezed in, half dressed, beautiful long olive skinned legs on show. She had come in from her bedroom which was just off the hallway, almost opposite the front room doorway. She walked past me, turned around, long hair flicked as she did so, the scent of her sweet body spray filling the room. She tossed her head back and, eyes rolled to the ceiling, said dramatically, "Mum I don't feel well," then strutted back out and into her room, closing her door behind her.

"Ok, just get to sleep now, it's late. If you need me, call me!" I called after her.

I thought nothing more of it. About ten minutes later, I could hear some banging coming from her room. It sounded like something heavy had fallen. I put down my laptop and headed across the hall towards her room, asking her if she was alright.

I opened the door.

She was on the floor, eyes rolling, silly grin on her face as if she was completely intoxicated. But I knew she wasn't drunk – for a start she hadn't touched alcohol yet, she was only twelve and secondly, she had been fine earlier in the evening, there was no way she could get that drunk that quick.

So what on earth was wrong with her?

I tried to get her up but she kept falling back, then she passed out on the bed. She was floppy, unable to sit or stand but kept making twitchy jerking movements. She was completely unresponsive; unable to talk or communicate and her eyes flitted between staring into space, being half closed and rolling to the back of her head. She was also making strange noises and was clearly distressed.

I was panicking and didn't know what was wrong with her, but knew she needed help. I had terrible mobile phone signal in the flat, so I ran back into the front room and frantically called my Mum from my landline.

I wasn't able to be with Riannon at the same time as the receiver was attached to the phone, so it was killing me that I had left her. Mum answered.

"Mum, Riannon's delirious!"

"What do you mean? Have you had a row?"

"No, it's as if she's drunk but she's not drunk!"

"I can't hear you properly. She's not well?"

"Oh my god Mum, I'm going to go and phone an ambulance!" I screamed.

Shaking and breathless I dialled 999.

I was so anxious as I couldn't see Riannon from where I was. When I got through, the panic in my voice had reached a shrill pitch.

"Please send an ambulance, there's something wrong with my daughter!" I screamed.

They asked me loads of questions, was she like this, was she like that, but I couldn't see her I didn't know.

"Please, just send an ambulance!" I pleaded.

I was on the phone for what seemed like ages, being asked questions when I just dropped the phone and ran back in the room.

She was completely unresponsive, making these strange jerking movements – was she having a fit?

I ran back to the phone, crying, my heart was racing. "Where's the ambulance?!" I screamed.

"It's on its way, please calm down."

Calm down?!

A good twenty minutes later, I saw a small ambulance car pull up outside.

It took it's time parking.

I went to the front door. A female paramedic sauntered

29

out the car, slowly got her kit out the back and casually made her way over towards me.

"Thank God you're here!" I cried, holding her arm to usher her in. "It's my daughter, she's through here!"

She stopped, turned to me, looked me square in the eye and said firmly, "Don't touch me."

I was confused. I thought for a moment. I was in a state of panic.

"I'm sorry" I said, taken aback. "Please, come this way?"

She paused for a second, then followed me into Riannon's room.

I led her in to my daughter's room where Riannon was lying on her side on the bed, completely unresponsive. The paramedic called her name, shone a light in her eyes and checked her pulse and vital signs.

"I found her like this about half an hour ago," I said. "It happened suddenly, she seemed fine all evening!" I explained.

As the paramedic attended to Riannon, my parents arrived. The paramedic explained that she felt certain it was nothing to worry about and asked us all to stay calm and be reassured that she was not overly concerned at this point. I left the room with my Mum and Dad so that the paramedic could focus on Riannon without any distractions.

I checked back in after about ten minutes.

"How is she doing? Does she need to go to hospital?" I asked. The paramedic was stroking Riannon's hair, as her head was resting on her lap. Riannon was still unresponsive, her eyes just staring into space, occasionally rolling to the back of her head.

"No, she does not need to go to hospital. Has she suffered any trauma recently?" asked the paramedic.

"Erm, it's been a tough year for her," I said. "I was very ill this time last year and she went to live with her nan and granddad for three months and more recently, she's been very upset over her Dads split with his girlfriend."

"I think this is psychological" said the paramedic. "An emotional response to something troubling her."

I was amazed at this conclusion. "Are you saying there is nothing wrong with her medically?" I asked.

"Yes. She is fine medically. Her observations are all fine, she is a good colour, her lips are not blue and she is fully conscious and aware of her movements."

"She looks semi-unconscious to me," I said.

"And her jerky movements look involuntary!"

The paramedic tried to reassure me that Riannon was fully in control and aware of her movements and reiterated that she was fine from a medical point of view.

I was astonished at her conclusion.

"Could she have unknowingly taken a substance while out with her friends this evening? Could someone have spiked her drink? Could she have fallen and knocked her head?" I asked, wracking my brains for an explanation.

The paramedic stated categorically that there was 'NO indication of substances' as her pupils were not dilated.

She was adamant that Riannon could talk and act 'normally' if she wanted to, but was choosing not to.

'This is ridiculous,' I thought.

"I'd like more time with her alone please, to try to get her to talk about what is upsetting her," said the paramedic. "In order to get to the bottom of this."

And so, she continued trying to get Riannon to speak.

"I really feel she needs to go to hospital!" I cried.

"Please let me do my job," she replied. I left the room again. Mum and I were so worried and Dad was trying to keep us calm.

A short while later, the paramedic called us back in to the room. "Have you seen these marks?" she asked, pointing to Riannon's wrists.

I stared in disbelief. Both wrists had dozens of little cuts on them, not fresh, maybe a few days old. She had clearly been self harming. Mum, Dad and I all stared at each other.

"We had no idea," I said. Thinking about it, she always wore a long sleeve cardigan, saying she was cold even though it was summer.

It had never crossed my mind she could have been doing this.

The paramedic was still trying to get Riannon to talk, even though she was clearly unresponsive. Mum suggested I phone Riannon's friend, who she had been playing out with earlier, to see if she could shed any light.

Her Mum answered.

"Hi it's Melanie, Riannon's Mum. I'm sorry to call so late but Riannon's unwell, we have a paramedic with her,

I need to speak to Bethany to see if anything happened at the park earlier."

Bethany's Mum asked me to hang on while she woke her. Bethany came to the phone. "Hi Mel, is Riannon OK?"

"Not really, I need to know if anyone gave her anything at the park, a drink, something to eat?"

"No."

"Did she fall, hit her head?"

"No."

"OK, what about these marks on her wrists, do you know anything about that?"

"Erm, I don't know if I should tell you."

"Bethany, this is serious. If you know something, you need to tell me."

And she did. She told me how Riannon had been self harming for about three months. I was shocked and devastated.

Three months ago was when her Dad and Karen split up. I told the paramedic.

It was now about 01.30am. Riannon was exactly the same; she had not improved in any way and had not talked to the paramedic.

"I'm going to write to the doctor so he has it first thing in the morning, strongly advising that Riannon is to have psychological assessment. Leave her to sleep, try to get some rest yourselves and take her to the doctors in the morning."

"PLEASE take her to hospital!" I pleaded again.

"Hospital is the LAST place she needs to be," said the paramedic firmly. "Look, I've been doing this job for many years - if I thought for one moment that a child needed to be in hospital I would not risk my job by not sending them."

"How are we going to get her in the car to get her to the doctors?" My Mum asked, "she's a dead weight!!"

"You could call the doctor out" replied the paramedic, "but there's every chance she'll be OK in the morning. Play it by ear."

And so she wished us all the best, assured us she would write to the doctor and left at about 02.00am. Dad went back to theirs to get Mum some pyjamas so she could stay the night on the sofa and I went to bed.

I hardly slept, but must have drifted off as I awoke at 06.00am to my Mum asking me to help her.

"Riannon's wet the bed," she said. "I'm having trouble cleaning her as she's a completely dead weight."

So I helped and we changed her clothes. She was still completely 'out of it.'

I made us both a cup of tea. We looked at the clock. "What time does your doctors open?" Mum asked. "8.00 I think, or half eight" I said. "Mind you, they'll probably not come out until after surgery," Mum said.

We both sat there on the sofa, waiting for the doctors to open so we could call.

"This is ridiculous!" I said after a few minutes, "I'm going to call the out of hours surgery!"

I explained that we had called a paramedic out a few hours earlier and that Riannon was still no better and that I was very concerned.

"OK, a paramedic is on the way," I was told.

Meanwhile, the person on the phone asked me if I had a defibrillator.

"What's that?" I wondered. "Mum, have we got a defibrillator?"

Mum looked utterly confused. "No" she replied, dismayed. "What a strange question! Ask them to ask the paramedic to bring one!"

Before too long, a male paramedic arrived at around 06.30am.

"Hello" he said, "I know all about Riannon and what's happened tonight as my colleague who attended earlier has handed everything over to me."

He entered Riannon's room. "Hi Riannon, can you answer me? I know you can hear me!"

He was in her room for a few minutes. I could see from where I was sitting in the front room that he had propped Riannon up against her headboard and was doing observations on her.

Riannon was still floppy and unresponsive.

"Come on, raise your arm for me!" he ordered, "I know you can do it!"

Nothing.

He came out of her room and joined me and my Mum in the front room.

"Shouldn't she be in hospital?" I asked for the umpteenth time that night.

"No, absolutely not" he replied. "My colleague was right not to send her last night and I'll not be sending her now."

I felt like I was stuck in a nightmare.

"This can't be happening," I thought.

"My daughter displays similar symptoms; it's a psychological problem. It's not uncommon," he said. "She is fully aware of what she's doing; it's not as if she has taken something to make her act in this way. She is consciously doing it."

"Well, if it's an act," I snapped, "she deserves an Oscar!"

Sensing my frustration, my Mum took over.

"Look, we're really concerned. She has never done anything like this before. She's not an attention-seeking child, she doesn't like fuss or to be 'the centre of attention.' We really don't feel that she's putting it on."

"She also wet herself in the night," Mum said, trying to find reasons to show that this was serious.

"Ahh," said the paramedic, "Now, that does tip things very slightly in favour of her going to hospital. It suggests she may have slipped into unconsciousness during the night, although this can also be *part of the act.*"

He said that because of the fact that she had wet herself, he would call for an ambulance, stating that there was a possibility of a 'urinary tract infection' although it was still highly likely to be psychological.

I was so relieved she would finally be going to hospital.

At about 6.50am, two more paramedics, a male and female, arrived in a proper ambulance. They spoke to the other paramedic and entered Riannon's room with Mum and I.

"Riannon, we need you to get up now, sit in this chair."

They had brought in a special chair to wheel her out

to the ambulance. Mum and I helped to move her from the bed over to the chair. The two new paramedics were also assisting her as it was clear that Riannon could not walk unaided.

I let go as my back gave way and she fell to the floor.

What happened next really upset me.

The woman shouted: "NOW GET UP CHILD! You're NOT a baby, you're twelve years old! You've hurt your Mum's back - what's wrong with you?!!?! Get up NOW!!!!!!"

I was mortified. With everyone's assistance - someone was heavy handed as she was left with bruises - Riannon made it onto the chair, still completely floppy and 'out of it.' She was wheeled into the ambulance and all three paramedics asked for a few minutes alone with her in the ambulance before I got in.

I said that was fine; I was just relieved she was finally going to hospital and my Mum and Dad prepared to follow in their car, behind.

The first man emerged from the ambulance after a few minutes and left in his vehicle, the woman walked round to the driver's side of the ambulance and the second man ushered me in the back of the ambulance with him, next to where Riannon was laying, strapped down and clearly distressed.

I held her hand and he stated quietly that 'she knew exactly what she was doing.' They had done a pinch test, which he explained would not be felt by someone who was semi or unconscious.

Riannon had reacted. He also told me that the way she had collapsed while they were trying to get her on the chair was obviously 'put on,' that when people 'really' faint/collapse, they don't do it in the manner she did. He even said to me, "Put it his way, we are not even going to hospital by blue light."

I did not know what to think, but watching my daughter twitching, jerking, making distressing noises and seeing her eyes roll to the back of my head was very concerning to me and I just wanted to get to hospital.

Once we arrived at the hospital and were seen by the consultant, they did the pinch test and deducted she was completely unresponsive.

I was asked if Riannon could have taken any substances.

The thought had never crossed my mind that she could have taken something intentionally. While they tested for a viral infection, brain scans etc, they asked us to search her room for tablets. Nothing showed in the tests that indicted a head injury or any kind of infection. They said it looked increasingly like an overdose, especially as she had become poorly so suddenly and without warning.

"But the paramedics checked her eyes and said the pupils were not dilated, indicating no substances," I said.

The consultant looked horrified.

"That is a myth" she said. "Recreational drugs dilate the pupils, but many prescription drugs do not."

The consultant was also amazed that, even following the discovery of her self-harming, the paramedics did not suspect an overdose and said that we should make a complaint against the paramedics who attended the scene to protect others from tragic outcomes.

I stayed with Riannon at the hospital while my Mum and Dad went to mine. My Mum found a packet of my prescription pills in her room at home - strong anti-psychotics which I had been prescribed a year ago.

Tests confirmed she had taken a massive overdose and was lucky to still be alive. We were told the next day to prepare for the worst; that she was in danger of having a seizure, internal problems, brain damage and death.

I was beside myself. I felt sick and light-headed.

Thankfully, she surprised everyone and made a remarkable recovery after five days, but how different things could have been.

My seemingly happy-go-lucky, bright, happy daughter had tried to kill herself. Why? I had to find out. What was happening that was so awful that she felt she had no way out? And as for the self harming, what was that all about? Why?

I wondered if she may be being abused.

I was grateful she was alive, but very worried that she would attempt suicide again; I remembered my own suicide attempt and how much I still wanted to die after coming round in hospital. I was only saved from a second attempt on my life by being admitted to a psychiatric hospital and being put on suicide watch.

All I knew was that we had to find out why she did this, so we could help her. But she wasn't talking. They got a social worker and psychiatrist to talk to her to try to find out why she did it. My family and I asked her gently too.

Nothing. All she said was that she didn't know why she did it and she was happy it didn't work.

That sounded familiar. That's exactly what I had said when I was put in front of the psychiatrist in hospital.

It was a lie. I wanted to be discharged so that I could jump in front of a train.

The psychiatrist bought her story.

"I think she genuinely is pleased it didn't work he said."

I wasn't convinced.

She was assigned a social worker, a school coordinator and a team at CAMHS (Child and Adolescent Mental Health Service). Her school were brilliant. They told me there were rumours spreading about her and the children were all really upset, so they were going to call a special assembly to explain what had happened and that she was OK.

Her friends made her cards and came to see her in hospital. Riannon did say to me she was surprised and touched by how many people cared about her. This surprised me as she was a very popular girl.

I asked them not to discharge her from hospital until we knew why she had done it – I was so scared that she would try it again unless we could find the reason why and help her. But they reassured me that she would be seen at home by a crisis team and said that I just had to keep a close eye on her.

She would soon start art therapy at CAMHS and they would try to find out. They asked me not to push for answers and that if I became worried that her life was danger, I was to take her to A&E.

I was on tenterhooks.

Riannon was discharged from hospital on the Friday. I threw away all my old medicines and kept what was needed under lock and key. Lots of people came to visit her in the following week - friends, family, various agencies, psychiatrists and doctors.

I tried gently speaking to her, saying that nothing she could possibly have done or thought would make me judge her or be angry with her. But she still wasn't talking. So I left it and didn't mention it again.

The school said she didn't need to come back until she felt ready, but she was keen to go back and see her friends and returned the following Monday.

I was so worried about her leaving my side. She had begun seeing a psychiatrist and doing art therapy with a trained counsellor, but neither had so far made any headway as to why she did what she did.

Melanie Burnell

Chapter Six

Riannon's Battle

One warm summer's night a few weeks later, Riannon came into my bed for a cuddle, which was quite rare as she wasn't overly affectionate.

She didn't say anything; she just cuddled up to me. She was sleepy but I could tell she had things on her mind.

"Ri, tell me why you did it," I said gently.

She got really upset. I hated seeing her so distressed but I pushed, as I felt she just might open up.

"No," she cried.

"Has someone been touching you?" I asked.

"No."

I was wracking my brains for possible reasons. What could it be? Some time ago she had said in a Facebook post that she was bisexual. I didn't think much of it at the time; I didn't think she even understood it! But could that be it?

"Do you prefer girls to boys? Is that it?"

"No Mum" she said getting a bit angry. She was shaking her head saying, "I can't tell you, I can't tell you!"

"Yes, you can," I gently coaxed.

"No, you're going to judge me, you're going to think I'm bad," she cried.

"I'm not, sweetheart, you can tell me, I can make it better. Whatever it is, we can fix it."

"No you can't."

She tried to leave, I pulled her close.

"Tell me," I whispered assertively.

She was very upset and looked terrified of admitting to what, quite clearly, was something very disturbing. Fighting back tears she said, "It's the voice inside my head."

"What voice?" I asked gently.

She explained that she had been hearing a very nasty, sarcastic voice inside her head for about a year. She cried and asked if I thought she was crazy. I said no and wiped her tears and hugged her.

I was shocked at what she had just told me, but so relieved that she had finally spoken about her reasons for trying to end her life. Now I knew what we were working with, I was certain she could be helped. I just needed to find out as much as possible so I could tell the team at CAMHS.

With my gentle questioning, she talked to me for a number of hours. She was very articulate throughout, as she calmly explained it all to me.

She didn't remember exactly when it started but thought it was after we returned home from my hospital stay a year ago. Thinking back, there was tons of help and support for me at that time, with various professionals always making sure I was OK, but no-one thought to find out how it had affected Riannon.

None of us had a clue that she was going through such turmoil.

She said the voice had become intolerable when her Dad and Karen split up a few months ago. It repeatedly told her that it was all her fault and that she was to blame for everyone's unhappiness. This was when she started self-harming, as a way to cope with it. She described it as a battle between her and the voice. She said she only won when she cut herself. It was always there trying to defeat her, mocking her, playing on her deepest thoughts and insecurities.

She had never heard of people hearing voices before and didn't know it could happen to others too. She felt very alone, like she was going crazy all this time. It must have been so very disturbing; I couldn't even begin to imagine how awful it must have been for her.

The voice was clear, nasty, negative, persistent and continuous. It was there all the time, apart from when she was sleeping, doing PE or when she was very focussed on something.

It would tell her relentlessly, "You are nothing, you are worthless. No one cares for you or loves you."

It would say different things to her each day based on her own thoughts or actions, usually sticking to one theme each day. She gave some examples of how it chose what to say – its aim was always to corrupt and upset her.

If she woke up, looked outside and thought, "It's a nice

sunny day, I think I'll wear a belly top and jeans today" then it would snipe, "God, don't you look fat! Look at your fat legs!" All day it would repeat, "You're fat, you're fat, don't eat that, you'll get fatter!" So she'd stop eating because she would think through its suggestion and conclude it was right.

If she had decided to play out with the boys, it would say, "You're a dirty worthless little slut aren't you?! SLAG! Hahaha!"

Whenever family or friends said nice things to her like "I love you" or "you're beautiful" the voice would say, "They don't mean it, look they are lying to you!"

It was repetitive to the point that she visualised what it was saying and then could not get the vision out of her head, of for example, her being fat, ugly or worthless. She then believed it. She said there was no let up. The voice knew all her weaknesses. She said she could not get away from it.

To be honest it sounded like a living nightmare.

I told her that I would help her get rid of it.

She looked away. I asked her if it said something. She said it told her immediately after, "I will never leave you."

I now realised that the way she looks away when I tell her I love her and fixes a small smile is not because she feels uncomfortable with my affection, but because inside her head, a voice she can't tell me about, is telling her, "It's not true."

How unbelievably cruel. The poor girl had been

46

bottling this up, trying to deal and cope with this for a year now. I had a huge amount of respect for her for that.

She visualised it as just being a mouth moving with no face. In tone she said it kind of sounded like her voice, but she wasn't sure. When it gets strong, then it gets deeper. If others are being mean to her, the voice feeds off that and gets louder and stronger which becomes unbearable.

She said a group of boys at school were picking on her recently and the voice got really loud. It changed into a deeper, man's voice. It felt like her head was going to explode like a scene out of Harry Potter. She had even banged her head off a wall and punched herself in a desperate attempt to stop it.

She also explained how she 'blanks out' or 'zones out' approximately once a day where everything kind of fades out and goes blurry, except for one thing that she zooms in and focuses on. Everything else grows fainter, including sound – she can't hear friends or teachers talk for example. Then after a few minutes, 'BOOM!' she's suddenly back again – it's like she snaps out of it. She thinks at this point that everyone is looking at her and knows she's going crazy. She described it as having a complete detachment from reality.

In fact, it had been noted in her recent school report that 'she sometimes day dreams.'

The voice was still there all the time; while she was eating, reading, playing a game on her phone, watching TV, at school, and playing with friends. She said she had

to make a lot of effort to play and do her work at school which she described as manageable but hard to describe.

Incredibly she had learned to deal with it to get through each day.

She said it pulls her away from finishing her work properly and then taunts her that nothing she ever does will be any good. I found it amazing how she had somehow learned to get by. She found it hard to explain how she was able to do her work. It was like she'd just focus and do it very quickly, I think. Luckily she was a bright girl so she could get away with that. But I wondered how much more she would be able to achieve in lessons without it.

She said matter-of-factly, "School work would be so much easier without it."

I bet it would.

When playing with her friends, she said she always tried to force a smile and join in but understandably she was not a care-free child and acting that was must be so hard.

She said she was able to sleep OK, but usually very late. She had her routine of watching two episodes of her favourite programme and then usually falls asleep during the next show.

She had clearly developed a way of coping but was desperately sad that she could not naturally be happy. She had to pretend a lot of the time. Also, whenever she did laugh, straight away it would tell her to stop. She said she liked running while listening to 'Eminem' as it made her feel like she was running away from it. Some songs made her feel better, but only certain songs and only for a short while.

She said she had talked to Bethany about her thoughts and feelings a bit, but had not told anyone about the voice until me tonight. She had wanted to talk to Mr Cheeseborough, a lovely teacher at school who she really liked, about the cutting, not long before her suicide attempt. But she couldn't go through with it. She said she fears for the future and worries that people will think she's crazy or insane.

I could relate to this, as that was how I felt when I was unwell.

She was confused about what the voice was. She thoughtfully pondered if it was real when I asked her. It was very real to her, but she was aware no one else could hear it. She described it as weird, as if the voice had now become a part of her. She was aware that it wasn't 'normal.'

"It doesn't tell me what to do or think, I make up my own mind," she told me adamantly. She explained that it doesn't tell her what to think and feel; rather it puts the suggestions in her mind then she thinks about it and believes it. She thinks through everything it says to her, trying to work out what 'she' really feels about something and what it's trying to make her feel. She is so very bright and tries to analyse these thoughts. It must literally do her head in. It must be so exhausting, depressing, confusing and disturbing yet she still manages to function.

Amazing.

I suggested she could start writing things down as a release and to try to make sense of what was going on in her mind. She said she hadn't in all this time for fear someone would find it. I couldn't say I blamed her. But now that she had told me, I wanted to encourage it. She was a very good writer – and speaker! She was describing this all so clearly.

She told me how she had started cutting herself with cola can ring pulls at school, then with razors at my parent's house whenever she could, every other day or so. She gave a very graphic account of the extreme sensual feelings of the voice leaving her body for the few minutes she would bleed. She said it felt like the life was draining away from her. She believed that spraying perfume on the wound would make sure that it was gone. The stinging helped her feel that she had won. She knew each time that it would return, but for around fifteen minutes it gave her a break.

After cutting she would stare at the mirror and tell it "bye!" and pull at her hair. It sounded like a very emotionally charged ritual. As she would walk away and head downstairs she would look at the cut marks then cover them up. Then, sure enough, the voice would return.

She really wanted to defeat it, but it always laughed, "Haha, I will defeat you!" At times at our home where no razor was to hand (it was kept in a cupboard), she would spray perfume into her mouth to get rid of the voice. She felt the perfume was significant to try to combat it.

I asked her if she still had thoughts of killing herself.

She said that she – or rather the voice – still had these thoughts every day. She has thoughts of running in front of a bus. For sometime before her suicide attempt, while walking home from school, she would count 1-2-3-4-5 then walk into the road, hoping to get knocked down.

She explained it was unbearable; the voice wanted to defeat her, so keeps putting these thoughts in her mind.

Melanie Burnell

Chapter Seven

Finally Free

On the Thursday, before the Monday that it happened, some boys at school in her science class were being really mean again (things had been bad for a while, each time their nasty words feeding the voice), but this time she had 'the worst experience of her life.'

The voice got so excruciatingly loud that her mind felt like it was going to explode. She had an intense pain in her head. She was panicking, shaking and crying inside and asked to go to the toilet. There she wanted to call out, but didn't want to draw attention to herself. She said it was unimaginable torture and she was screaming inside. She banged her head off the wall so hard to stop the pain and loud voice in her head. The voice stopped. She tried to calm herself down, wiped away her tears and returned to class.

For the rest of the day, she thought she had defeated it.

Thursday evening blurred into Friday and then the weekend. Sadly the voice returned on that Monday. That afternoon, while at the park she saw Craig, a boy from school and began feeling incredibly guilty for some reason,

thinking that she had made him feel bad even though he had been so mean to her of late.

The voice would not let up. When she returned home, she shut her bedroom door and paced around in a state while the voice laughed at her and mocked her. She got a nasty text from Craig, saying she should kill herself and cut herself some more. I gathered that some of the children from school knew about the self harming.

She could no longer bear the voice inside her head and went to the kitchen cupboard to get some pills to end her life. She came across paracetamol first, but put them back as she didn't think they would do anything as they were 'just used for headaches.'

I couldn't help but think how different things could have been had she taken those. Then she found a packet of my pills from when I was just out of hospital – high dose anti-psychotics which I came off soon after, so there were lots left in the packet. She thought these must be strong, so she took them into her room.

Quick-thinking, cutting and sharp as ever, the voice taunted her as she took them one by one. She only stopped when she began to feel sick. She felt regret almost immediately after, but then felt a sense of peace as she felt that, although it had finally defeated her, she would be free.

She remembers waking up in hospital and being a bit disorientated. As she recovered more the next day, she remembered what she had done. Interestingly, the next three days that she was awake in hospital, for the first time in almost a year, she did not have the voice. She felt genuinely relieved that her attempt to end her life had not worked and was touched by how much her friends and family cared.

All that weekend, now back at home, the voice stayed away and she thought she had killed it! Then, when back at school the following Monday – one week after her overdose – suddenly and without warning it came back during her science lesson.

Everything went blurry; she was so scared, and it said, "I'm back!"

We'd been talking for hours. I stroked her head, kissed her on the cheek and tucked my covers around her. "Get some sleep, well done for opening up sweetheart. I promise you we will defeat it, OK?"

She closed her eyes, I switched off the side lamp and headed down the hallway to the kitchen. I looked at the clock. It was almost 2am.

I put the kettle on, made a cup of coffee and took out my lined notebook from the kitchen draw. My head was spinning with all that Riannon had just told me and I knew I had to write it all out, ready to show her psychiatrist, social worker and the school the next day.

The professionals needed to know this information in order to help her. Scared my memory would let me down and feeling emotionally and physically exhausted, I sat at the table in the front room and began getting it all down on paper.

I stayed up for two more hours, writing 15 sides of A4. Relieved I had got as much down as I could remember,

I went to bed, cuddling Riannon, determined to get her the right treatment and feeling positive that she would make a full recovery.

The next morning, I told her that I needed to tell the man at CAMHS what she had told me so that he could help her. She looked horrified.

"I don't want anyone to know" she said, looking upset. I explained why we needed to tell him.

"Ok" she said, "But please don't tell anyone else including Nana."

I really wanted to tell my Mum, but she begged me not to until after we had seen the psychiatrist. I found this hard, as I wanted Mum to know, but I respected her wishes and when she phoned asking how Riannon was, I didn't tell her what I'd found out.

I needed Riannon to trust me.

After she left for school, I drove down to the post office and photocopied the dossier, putting each copy in a named envelope. I then drove to CAMHS, telling the receptionist I needed to urgently speak with Riannon's psychiatrist. She asked me to leave the envelope for him and that would get him to phone me shortly

The psychiatrist phoned me to say he had read the dossier and wanted to speak to Riannon and I in light of this new information that afternoon after school. I was very optimistic that she would get better now.

When Riannon came in from school, I explained that we were going to go to CAMHS to see the man who would help make her better. She looked unhappy.

"It'll be fine, I promise."

I drove to my Mums next and told her everything. I made her read a copy of what I had written the night before, as it was important to me that she knew the details. She was shocked and concerned at what she had learned, but relieved that Riannon had finally opened up and praised me for getting her to talk.

I phoned the school and Riannon's social worker to tell them too. I wanted all the people involved in Riannon's care to know what we were dealing with. Everyone was very empathetic and a meeting at CAMHS was arranged for us all the next day.

Riannon was to continue with art therapy and counselling and was prescribed Fluoxetine, an anti-depressant ideal for children.

I was relieved she was having some medication, therapy and counselling and felt hopeful she would come through this.

Melanie Burnell

Chapter Eight

Difficult Times

The next few weeks were a whirlwind of meetings and emotions.

As with me, once things had hit crisis point i.e. a suicide attempt, there was so much help and support. It made me wonder why things have to get so bad in order to get into the system.

Riannon was one of the lucky ones to have survived and be getting all this help and I prayed that she would soon get better. A weird thing happened to me during this time – I became 'manic.' Not that I was aware of this, my care-coordinator Beatrice picked up on it.

I was talking very fast, jumping from one subject to another and having lots of business ideas. It was quite bizarre, my brain was firing on all cylinders, I felt like I didn't need much sleep and was 'wired.' The stress of everything had made me manic! The doctor came out and prescribed me some medication and within a few days I was in a much more 'normal' state. They said I was lucky I responded so quickly, otherwise I could have been put back in hospital!

A year later, I was diagnosed with bi-polar as I had had one 'down' which was my psychotic breakdown and now one 'up', which was my manic episode. My family and friends were not surprised with the diagnosis, as I am quite 'all or nothing' as a person and have always been a bit 'up or down.'

I'm glad I have only ever had these two main episodes though and work hard to stay well and keep away from stress as much as possible, as that is my trigger.

* * *

It was during my mania that I had an awful car crash on the way to visit Riannon, who was on suicide watch in hospital.

I had found a screwed up suicide note while cleaning her bedroom one evening which said 'Dear... I'm sorry but the voice has finally defeated me. I tried to overcome it but it beat me. Sorry, Riannon.'

I was beside myself, she was at Youth Club and I didn't know if she was going to do something that night, or what. So, I rang her friend's Mum who was due to collect her, screaming: "Please go and get her and make sure she's OK!!" Meanwhile, I drove like a madman to Mum and Dads, tears streaming down my face desperate to show them the note and come up with a plan to get her to go into hospital as I knew A&E was our only option now.

I pulled up on their drive and rang her friend's Mum again who reassured me Riannon was fine; she was bringing her back soon. "Please bring her to my Mum's," I asked, which she said she would.

Once inside, I told my parents everything.

"Right," said Mum. "Let's tell her that we are going there for a meeting with CAMHS, otherwise we'll never get her there!"

"Good idea." I quickly phoned the hospital to explain that we would be bringing her in, but not to question us when we get to reception, so she wouldn't suspect anything until we were actually seen.

With that, Riannon knocked on the door.

"Hi sweetheart! We're just off to a meeting at the hospital with CAMHS. Come on, let's go!"

"Oh god, I really don't want to, I'm tired!" she cried.

We persuaded her and reluctantly she got in the car with us. As we arrived, my heart was in my mouth. Things were serious. They NEEDED to take us seriously. I prayed they would refer Riannon to a special children's hospital where she would get the care she needed before she made an attempt on her life again.

We walked up to reception. "We're here for a meeting" I said. "It's for Riannon Burnell."

The receptionist nodded. "This way, please."

We entered a room where a doctor came to see us.

"What's been going on?" he asked.

I pulled the note from my pocket and looked at Riannon.

"Sorry sweetheart, I found this note and had to get you here."

She got really angry and upset, saying she had written

it some time ago in case things all got too much. I just hoped the doctor would take us seriously.

He did.

I explained how worried I was that she wanted to die and he agreed that she should be kept in overnight and assessed. I was so relieved.

Riannon was scared. I explained that she would get better and that we were all here to help make that happen. She was put on a children's ward and we stayed for a while and were then told we had to go home, but could return the next day.

* * *

The next morning, I got in the car and zoomed over to the hospital.

It was absolutely chucking down with rain and I was going far too fast for the conditions. I lost control and skidded into a tree going about 70mph! BANG!!! The car shot up in the air and spun round 180 degrees. The airbags came out and the gears went through the floor.

I saw my life flash before me and really thought I had died. I got out as quickly as I could, afraid the car would blow up and limped to the side of the road. I knew my arm was broken, my chest hurt and my knee was throbbing.

I got my phone from my pocket and tried to unlock it to dial 999, but couldn't unlock it. I was disorientated, in pain and scared but relieved that I wasn't dead or seriously injured.

I sat on the bank and put my knee in the puddle next to it as the cool water made it hurt less. The rain was coming down so hard, I was drenched.

Cars stopped and people got out to help. An ambulance arrived and I was given gas and air, which I liked! They took me to the hospital where I called my Mum. She couldn't believe what had happened and the irony that she now had both myself and Riannon in hospital.

Her and Dad visited me and reassured me that Riannon was OK. I had broken and dislocated my arm and was in a world of pain, but just wanted to see Riannon. When I finally got to see her, she gave me a big cuddle and we fell asleep together on the hospital bed.

* * *

Riannon stayed in hospital for a few days.

They talked about moving her to a specialist children's psychiatric hospital, but decided against it as they felt it wouldn't be the best place for her. She was sent home but under the crisis care team, so we had a visit every day from someone.

Life was tough. I couldn't do much for myself, let alone Riannon as my arm was broken, so Mum said she would look after her while it healed. While Riannon was staying at Mums, her behaviour got worse and Mum was referred to a special person who teaches you how to discipline children. She worked really hard with the lady there who she got on well with. She supported Mum to support Riannon.

Meanwhile, I was getting phone calls from school every other day with upsetting news. My heart would sink each time the phone rang.

She was breaking into pencil sharpeners to use the blades to self harm. She had taken explicit photos of herself and sent them to a boy who had passed them onto his friends and so on. She was assigned someone special who put her on a course on internet safety following this.

She was smoking.

Poor behaviour/anger.

Toxic friendships.

She went away with her Dad and his family for a short UK caravan holiday where, during this time, she sneaked out at night to meet boys and smoke drugs. I was so worried about her behaviour, it was out of control and Mum and I didn't know what to do. We just kept implementing what Mum was learning from the behavioural lady and Riannon kept going to therapy.

We hoped for a miracle.

Riannon's psychiatrist explained that she had elements of different psychological disorders including PTSD (Post Traumatic Stress Disorder), the beginnings of an eating disorder, depression and psychosis. I knew she was getting treatment, but I didn't know how or when she would get better. He said that, although she was ahead of her years academically, she was emotionally a few years behind.

This made a lot of sense to me.

Then, one Saturday evening, she had gone to stay overnight at her Dad's place. He lived at the top of a twenty story high rise block of flats. She had tried to ring me early Sunday morning, but I hadn't heard my phone. So next she rang my Mum, who was running late for the gym so luckily, was there and answered.

"Nana, I've done something silly. Dad's gone out to the shops and I've cut a hole in the netting on the balcony and was going to jump off."

Calmly, Mum replied: "Where are you now sweetheart?"

"I'm still on the balcony."

"Ok, well turn around and walk inside sweetheart."

She said she doesn't know how she stayed so calm.

Meanwhile she ushered my Dad out of bed and told him to get dressed and go round there, explaining what had happened and that Jamie, her Dad, wasn't there.

My Mum kept Riannon talking the whole time until Dad arrived, who got there the same time as Jamie, who had no idea what was going on.

He was really angry and yelled at her. My Dad took her back home to his.

What a nightmare this all was.

Melanie Burnell

Chapter Nine

A Changing Tide

When my arm had healed a few weeks later, Riannon came back to live with me.

We all pulled together as a family and the psychiatry team, social services and the school were all still involved with her care. I resisted the urge to keep asking if the voice had gone yet but gradually, I could see she was healing.

She was recovering, getting better. Bit by bit, day by day. When the psychiatrist felt the time was right, he began weaning her off the medication. Her art therapy came to a close and she talked more with a wonderful counsellor called Dee, who she really liked.

Over time, she started seeing her less and less frequently. And then, almost as suddenly as it all started, it had stopped. She was back to her old lovely, happy self.

The voice had gone. She was free.

* * *

After about 16 months Riannon had come through it all and my, what strength of character did she now have.

She was almost 14, top of her class at school, popular, bright and happy again. Oh and did I mention beautiful?

She had a beauty that was almost untouchable, not only because of her physical elfin-like features, but because of what she had been through. She was strong, tough and oh, so beautiful. I had so much respect for her. I watched her shine bright as, piece by piece, she put her life back together.

It was a miracle!

* * *

Now 17, she's learning to drive, studying Law, Psychology and Business at sixth form after getting great GCSE results, she works as a waitress at a golf club and has a 20-strong group of friends both boys and girls, who are all absolutely lovely – they do things like go out for breakfast together – it's so sweet.

She values her home and family, helping out and being kind, and has developed a real love of cooking.

She likes going to festivals and generally enjoying being young! She's very sensible though, doesn't touch drugs and doesn't (usually!) drink too much. She's a great friend and is valued by all her friends, who recently made such a fuss of her for her birthday that she was in tears with all the balloons and presents and cards they gave to her.

She has also applied to be Head Girl at her school and I honestly couldn't be prouder. Here is what she wrote on her application:

"
I would like the opportunity to run for Head Girl. I consider the role of great importance as she has the opportunity to inspire and change many. A great role model I have in my life is my granddad who is the main reason I'm inspired to run for Head Girl. He was Head Boy for his school and has achieved many great things in his lifetime and I hope becoming Head Girl is my first step into the same direction as him.

I have always been academic; however I did go through a stage many years ago that I'm not proud of where my behaviour was not good due to my anger and disruptiveness. With the help of the school especially The Hub – which I believe is an amazing facility for young people – I was able to turn my behaviour around dramatically and better myself and I am so grateful for the help. I am now in the Top Performers of Year 12 which I personally feel is well deserved. I also love helping others including students and teachers whenever I can as making others happy is a big importance in my life.

I am really proud of my achievements over the years and believe there will be many more. I love being part of the school community and would love to be more involved as Head Girl. I would ensure to be an ambassador, someone who inspires other young people that you can better yourself and help them get out of any bad situations they find themselves in as I'm very understanding. I ultimately feel that I have a responsibility to give back to the people who helped me change my life so much. Influencing fellow students to be the best they can be is important to me as I believe everyone has a chance to succeed. I have great organisational skills which I see as one of my strengths. I would like to be seen as an approachable Head Girl, someone who others feel comfortable to talk to about anything.

I also want to inject an element of fun to show that working hard can be rewarding in lots of other ways. I have a part time job as a waitress in a gold club. I also help my manager with off-site functions such as weddings and parties which ultimately I believe has helped my confidence grow even further! It has also given me a sense of responsibility and I enjoy working with others as part of a tram. My boss says I am always hard working, punctual, reliable and friendly which is the same feedback I got from Mercedes-Benz where I did my work experience in Year 10 which also gave me some amazing skills I still use today.

I am looking to volunteer at the local Brownies and also at a soup kitchen over the next few months which I am looking forward to. I have received my inspiration for volunteering from my Auntie who is a charity ambassador. I would enjoy organising and being part of activities as well as promoting school life and providing a positive image to benefit the school. I would like to thank you for this opportunity and I hope you see that I am perfect for the role of Head Girl."

As for me, I finally met and married the man of my dreams in August 2017, Lee, where Riannon was Chief Bridesmaid. And the three of us live together happily, in our little home with this a little plaque hanging in the kitchen which says…

Love Grows Best in Little Houses
With Fewer Walls to Separate.
Where You Eat and Sleep so Close Together
You Can't Help but Communicate.
And if we had More Room Between us,
Think of all we'd Miss.
Love Grows Best in Houses Just Like This.

I'm so very excited for Riannon's future.

She has plans to go to university in Hawaii, live in Canada, get married and become a forensic accountant. And you know what? I believe in her and that whatever she wants, she will work hard to get.

I love her so very much and could not be prouder or more relieved at how she has come through so much at such a young age.

I hope she's an inspiration to many.

And when you become a diamond, you'll see why life had to pressure you.

Afterword

Kelly and I were privileged to take ownership of Live It Ventures LTD and by default, Live it Publishing and Britain's Next Bestseller in the October of 2016 from, the wonderful, Murielle Maupoint..

We inherited many amazing, talented and inspirational authors, but Melanie Burnell was something different. A survivor in her own right, Kelly and I were only able to get to know here via her debut novel (mentioned in this book), "The Day My Brain Slipped Out of my Head...' (fantastic title!) and it was a humbling experience.

Both myself and Kelly have our own experiences with mental health, be they family or personal and know that every incidence is both relative and unique. You cannot judge and compare one person's experiences to another; each individual has their own journey and challenges to face and hopefully, overcome.

Reading Melanie's first book was a privilege, as you are given a personal and very honest account of a woman with her own mental health problems and how she overcame them. Melanie is honest, has no shame or fear admitting those human emotions and characteristics that can be highlighted as the most fragile in such dark times. Yet she does it with courage, bravery and above all, humour.

'And When You Become a Diamond' is another such

book, only the focal point of this one is her daughter, Riannon. Once again, you step into someone's life and experience everything they did; the sadness, the fear and the strength to learn, grow and become a beacon for others who may be suffering something similar or different.

Mental health as a topic and in our society is still treated as some sort of affliction that should be ignored or dismissed. So many organisations and individuals do and are doing so much to move that ignorance and attitude forward, out of the dark where it has been historically kept out of fear and into the light.

Mental health isn't something that should be shoved to the back of the cupboard in the hopes it will go away; it should be embraced and that person nurtured, so that they to can feel the sun on their face and know that they are not different, they are just a human being who isn't perfect, is fragile, breakable and fixable.

Melanie Burnell's journey and that of her daughter, should be read by anyone with an interest in mental health and those who simply wish to learn and understand more.

Not many books allow you to step inside someone's life and see what they saw, feel what they felt.

It is a most humbling and honoured of privileges. Kelly and I are so very proud to have been allowed to play a small part in this book's journey to publication.

We hope you will feel the same. Best wishes,

David and Kelly McCaffrey

Directors
Live It Ventures LTD/Britain's Next Bestseller

About the Author

Melanie Burnell is the author of The Day My Brain Slipped Out of My Head and onto the Kitchen Floor; A journey through psychosis.

This is Melanie's second book.

Printed in Great Britain
by Amazon